Success With

Reading Comprehension

SCHOLASTIC

Editor: Ourania Papacharalambous
Cover design by Tannaz Fassihi; cover illustration by Kevin Zimmer
Interior design by Cynthia Ng
Interior illustrations by Aaron Blecha; all other photos © Shutterstock.com

ISBN 978-1-338-79860-9
Scholastic Inc., 557 Broadway, New York, NY 10012
Copyright © 2022 Scholastic Inc.
All rights reserved. Printed in the U.S.A.
First printing, January 2022
2 3 4 5 6 7 8 9 10   40   29 28 27 26 25 24 23

INTRODUCTION

Reading can be fun when high-interest stories are paired with puzzles, brain teasers, and fun activities. Parents and teachers alike will find *Scholastic Success With Reading Comprehension* to be a valuable educational tool. It is designed to help students in the third grade improve their reading comprehension skills. Students will practice finding the main idea and details, making inferences, following directions, drawing conclusions, and sequencing. They are also challenged to develop vocabulary, understand cause and effect, distinguish between fact and opinion, and learn about story elements. On page 4, you will find a list of the key skills covered in the activities throughout this book. Practicing and reviewing these important reading skills will help students become better readers. Remember to praise them for their efforts and successes!

TABLE OF CONTENTS

Grade-Appropriate Skills Covered in *Scholastic Success With Reading Comprehension: Grade 3*

Ask and answer questions to demonstrate understanding of a text, referring explicitly to the text as the basis for the answers.

Recount stories, including fables, folktales, and myths from diverse cultures; determine the central message, lesson, or moral and explain how it is conveyed through key details in the text.

Describe characters in a story and explain how their actions contribute to the sequence of events.

Determine the meaning of words and phrases as they are used in a text, distinguishing literal from nonliteral language.

Explain how specific aspects of a text's illustrations contribute to what is conveyed by the words in a story.

Determine the main idea of a text; recount the key details and explain how they support the main idea.

Describe the relationship between a series of historical events, scientific ideas or concepts, or steps in technical procedures in a text, using language that pertains to time, sequence, and cause and effect.

Determine the meaning of general academic and domain-specific words and phrases in a text relevant to a *grade 3 topic or subject area*.

Know and apply grade-level phonics and word analysis skills in decoding words.

Read with sufficient accuracy and fluency to support comprehension.

Read grade-level text with purpose and understanding.

Demonstrate command of the conventions of standard English grammar and usage when writing or speaking.

Demonstrate command of the conventions of standard English capitalization, punctuation, and spelling when writing.

Use knowledge of language and its conventions when writing, speaking, reading, or listening.

Determine or clarify the meaning of unknown and multiple-meaning words and phrases based on grade 3 reading and content, choosing flexibly from a range of strategies.

SQ3R

Do you know about SQ3R? It is a formula to help you understand what you read. It can be useful for any reading assignment. SQ3R is especially helpful when you are reading a textbook, like your social studies or science book. Each letter of the formula tells you what to do.

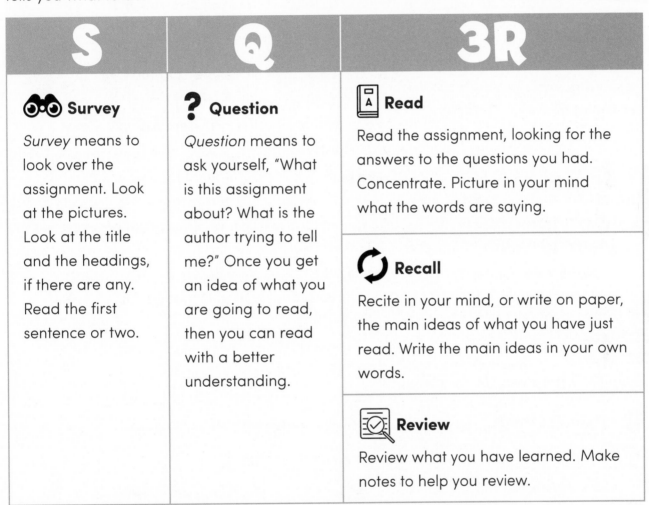

S	Q	3R
👀 **Survey**	❓ **Question**	📖 **Read**
Survey means to look over the assignment. Look at the pictures. Look at the title and the headings, if there are any. Read the first sentence or two.	*Question* means to ask yourself, "What is this assignment about? What is the author trying to tell me?" Once you get an idea of what you are going to read, then you can read with a better understanding.	Read the assignment, looking for the answers to the questions you had. Concentrate. Picture in your mind what the words are saying.
		🔄 **Recall**
		Recite in your mind, or write on paper, the main ideas of what you have just read. Write the main ideas in your own words.
		🔍 **Review**
		Review what you have learned. Make notes to help you review.

Now you have a valuable study tool. Use it to help study for a test. Use it to help remember what you read. Use it to help understand important information.

Let's practice. Read the assignment on the next page. Use the SQ3R formula step by step.

The Invention of the Telephone

Alexander Graham Bell was a teacher of the deaf in Boston. At night, he experimented with different ways to send messages over distances using a telegraph. Once when the metal in the telegraph stuck, Bell's assistant plucked the metal to loosen it. Bell, who was in another room, heard the sound in his receiver. He understood that the vibrations of the metal had traveled down the electric current to the receiver. He continued to work on this idea.

Alexander Graham Bell making a call.

On March 7, 1876, Alexander Graham Bell was awarded the first U.S. patent for the telephone. Three days later, he successfully spoke to his assistant over a telephone line. He was about to test a new transmitter when he spilled some battery acid on his clothes. He cried out to his assistant who was in another room, "Mr. Watson, come here! I want to see you!" Watson heard every word clearly on the telephone and rushed into the room.

Bell showed his invention to many people. Over time, more and more telephone lines were installed, and people began to use the invention in their homes and businesses.

Did SQ3R help you? Let's find out.

1 Who was awarded the first U.S. patent for the telephone? _____

_____

2 What did Mr. Bell say to Mr. Watson during the first telephone conversation?

_____

3 Who was Mr. Watson? _____

4 How did people first learn about the telephone? _____

_____

The Milky Way

What do you think of when you hear "Milky Way"? It's our galaxy! A galaxy is a grouping of stars. Scientists have learned that there are many galaxies in outer space. The Milky Way is a spiral-shaped galaxy with swirls of stars spinning out from the center. Some scientists believe there are hundreds of billions of stars in the Milky Way. One of those stars is the sun. Several planets, including Earth, orbit the sun. On a clear night away from city lights, you can see part of the Milky Way. It is called that because so many stars close together look like a milky white stripe across the sky. However, if you looked at it with a telescope, you would see that it is made up of many, many stars.

> The **main idea** of a story tells what the story is mostly about. **Details** in a story tell more information about the main idea.

Complete the main idea and details about the story.

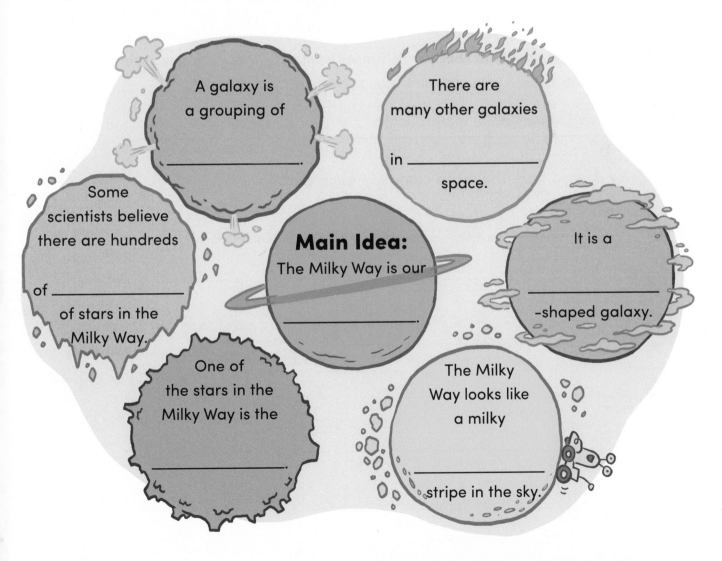

A galaxy is a grouping of

_____ .

There are many other galaxies

in _____

space.

Some scientists believe there are hundreds

of _____

of stars in the Milky Way.

Main Idea:
The Milky Way is our

_____ .

It is a

_____

-shaped galaxy.

One of the stars in the Milky Way is the

_____ .

The Milky Way looks like a milky

_____

stripe in the sky.

Wagon Train

In the spring of 1880, Will and Kate and their family left Pennsylvania and joined a wagon train headed for California. For months, their only home was the wagon. Each day Kate and Will

gathered wood as they walked beside the wagon. In the evening when the wagons stopped, Kate and her mother built a campfire for cooking supper. When it rained for several days, the roads were so muddy that the wagons got stuck. There was always the danger of snakes and bad weather. There were rivers and mountains to cross. There was no doctor to take care of those who got sick or injured. Traveling with a wagon train was a great adventure, but it was a very hard life.

Unscramble the words to make a complete sentence that tells the main idea.

wagon dangerous. on a Life hard and was train

_____

Choose a word from the list to complete each detail.

1 ___ ___ ___ ___ ___ ___ ___ ___ ___ wood

2 ___ ___ ___ ___ ___ ___ ___ over a campfire

3 ___ ___ ___ ___ ___ ___ for the rain to stop

4 ___ ___ ___ ___ ___ ___ ___ out for snakes

5 ___ ___ ___ ___ ___ ___ ___ rivers and mountains

6 ___ ___ ___ ___ ___ ___ sick or hurt with no doctor to help

| getting |
| gathering |
| waiting |
| crossing |
| cooking |
| watching |

What a Nose!

An elephant's trunk is probably the most useful nose in the world. Of course, it is used for breathing and smelling, like most noses are. However, elephants also use their trunks like arms and hands to lift food to their mouths. They suck water into their trunks and pour it into their mouths to get a drink. An adult elephant can hold up to four gallons of water in its trunk. Elephants can use their trunks to carry heavy things, such as logs that weigh up to 600 pounds! The tip of the trunk has a little knob on it that the elephant uses like a thumb. An elephant can use the "thumb" to pick up something as small as a coin. Trunks are also used for communication. Two elephants that meet each other touch their trunks to each other's mouth, kind of like a kiss. Sometimes a mother elephant will calm her baby by stroking it with her trunk. Can your nose do all those things?

Find the statement below that is the main idea of the story. Write _M.I._ next to it. Then find the details of the story. Write _D_ next to each detail. Be careful! There is one sentence that does not belong.

_____ **1** Elephants use their trunks to greet each other, like giving a kiss.

_____ **2** Elephants have very useful noses.

_____ **3** Mother elephants calm their babies by stroking them with their trunks.

_____ **4** Elephants use their noses for smelling and breathing.

_____ **5** Elephants can carry heavy things with their trunks.

_____ **6** Giraffes are the tallest animals in the world.

_____ **7** Elephants use their trunks to eat and drink.

The Math Contest

Story elements are the different parts of a story.
- The characters are the people, animals, or animated objects in the story.
- The setting is the place and time in which the story takes place.
- The plot of the story includes the events and often includes a problem and a solution.

Every Friday, Mr. Jefferson, the math teacher, held a contest for his students. Sometimes they played math baseball. Sometimes they had math relays with flash cards. Other times, they were handed a sheet of paper with a hundred multiplication problems on it. The student who finished fastest with the most correct answers won the contest. One Friday, there was a math bee. It was similar to a spelling bee, except the students worked math problems in their heads. There was fierce competition, until finally, everyone was out of the game except Riley and Rhonda. Mr. Jefferson challenged them with problem after problem, but both students continued to answer correctly every time. It was almost time for class to end, so Mr. Jefferson gave them the same difficult problem. They had to work it in their heads. Riley thought hard and answered, "20." Rhonda answered "18." Finally they had a winner. Riley was correct!

Answer the questions below about the story.

1 Name the three people in the story.

_____, _____, and _____

2 Where does the story takes place?
  ◯ in the gym   ◯ in the cafeteria   ◯ in Mr. Jefferson's classroom

3 What is the problem in the story?
  ◯ Mr. Jefferson held the contest on Thursday.
  ◯ Class was almost over, and the contest was still tied.
  ◯ Riley and Rhonda both answered correctly.

4 Who answered the last question correctly? _____

The Lake Cabin

As you read the paragraph, imagine the scene that the words are describing. In the picture below, draw everything that has been left out. Color the picture.

My favorite thing to do in the summer is to go to Grandpa's lake cabin. In the evening after a full day of fishing, Grandpa and I sit on the porch and enjoy the scenery. The sun setting behind the mountain fills the blue sky with streaks of orange and yellow. Colorful sailboats float by us in slow motion. Suddenly a fish jumps out of the water, making tiny waves in rings. A deer walks to the edge of the water to get a drink. Red and yellow flowers grow near the big rock. On the shore across the lake, we see a couple of tents. Someone must be camping there. A flock of geese flies over the lake in the shape of a V. Every time we sit and look at the lake, Grandpa says, "This is the best place on Earth!"

On another sheet of paper, write a paragraph describing the place that you think is "the best place on Earth." Read your paragraph to a friend.

Best Friends

Amy dreaded recess every day. She did not have any friends to play with. All the girls in her class were paired up with a best friend or in groups, and she always felt left out. So, instead of playing with anyone, Amy just walked around by herself. She wanted to seesaw, but that is something you need to do with a friend. She liked to swing, but she could not go very high. She wished someone would push her to get her started.

One day, the teacher, Mrs. Gibbs, walked up and put her arm around Amy. "What's the matter, Amy? Why don't you play with the other children?" she asked kindly.

Amy replied, "Everyone has a friend except me. I don't have anyone." Mrs. Gibbs smiled and said, "Amy, the way to get a friend is to be a friend." Amy asked, "How do I do that?"

Mrs. Gibbs answered, "Look around the playground. There are three classes of third-graders out here during this recess time. Find someone who is alone and needs a friend. Then go to that person and ask them to play." Amy said she would think about it, but she was afraid she would be too embarrassed. She wasn't sure she could do it.

The next day, Amy noticed a dark-haired girl all alone on the playground. She worked up her courage and walked over to the girl. "Hi! My name is Amy. Do you want to play with me?" she asked.

"Okay," the girl said shyly. As they took turns pushing each other on the swings, Amy found out that the girl's name was Ming. She and her family had just moved from China. She did not know anyone and could not speak much English yet. She needed a friend.

"Want to seesaw?" Amy asked. Ming looked puzzled. Amy pointed to the seesaw. Ming smiled and nodded. Amy was so happy. She finally had a friend!

On each blank, write the letter of the picture that correctly answers the question.

1 Where does this story take place? _____

2 Who is the main character in the story? _____

Who are the other two characters in the story? _____ and _____

3 What is the problem in the story? _____

4 What is Ming's problem? _____

5 How are Amy's and Ming's problems solved? _____

A. Mrs. Gibbs

B. playground

C. Ming needed a friend, too.

D. Ming

E. Amy

F. Amy asked Ming to play, and they became friends.

G. Amy needed a friend.

The Tallest Trees

Redwood trees are the tallest trees in the world. Some grow over 300 feet high, which is taller than a 30-story building. Think of it this way: If a six-foot-tall man stood at the base of a redwood tree, the tree would be 50 times taller than the man! These giant trees grow near the **coast** of California and Oregon. The **climate** is foggy and rainy there, which gives the redwoods a **constant** supply of water. Redwoods can grow for hundreds of years; in fact, some have lived for over 2,000 years! The reddish-brown **bark** is very thick, protecting the trees from insects, **disease**, and fires. Redwood trees are very important to the lumber companies because the trees are so large that each one can be cut into lots of **lumber**. Many of the trees are protected by law in Redwood National Park. Lumber companies cannot cut trees that grow there. This is so the trees will not become **extinct**.

Put an X beside the correct definition of each bolded word in the story.

1 **coast**   _____ land by the sea   _____ a desert

2 **climate**   _____ time   _____ weather

3 **constant**   _____ happens regularly   _____ never happens

4 **bark**   _____ leaves   _____ outer covering of trees

5 **disease**   _____ illness   _____ high temperatures

6 **lumber**   _____ plastic pipes   _____ wood cut into boards

7 **extinct**   _____ no longer existing   _____ expensive

Let's Play Soccer!

Soccer is the world's most popular sport. It is played in many countries all over the world. Every four years, an international competition is held. It is called the World Cup.

A **soccer field** is rectangular with a goal on each end. Each **goal** is made of a rectangular, frame-covered net. The game is played with a **soccer ball**.

Two teams compete against each other. One point is awarded to a team when it scores a goal. Whichever team scores the most goals wins the game.

There are 11 players on each team. **Forwards** have the most responsibility to score goals. Sometimes forwards are called strikers. They are helped by teammates who play at midfield. These players are sometimes called halfbacks. **Halfbacks** help to score goals and try to keep the other team's ball away from the goal. Other teammates play farther back on the field to defend their goal. They try to keep the other team from getting close enough to score. They are sometimes called **fullbacks**. Each team has one **goalie** whose job is to keep the other team from scoring by blocking the ball or catching it before it goes into the goal. A goalie may catch or throw the ball, but no other players may use their hands. They may use their feet, legs, chest, or head to move the ball. A referee will penalize a team if any players other than the goalie use their hands. Soccer is definitely a team sport. All the positions are important in winning the game.

Label the diagram using the bolded words from the story.

Scrambled Sentences

The sentences below are scrambled. Number them in the correct sequence.

> **Sequencing** means putting the events of a story in the order in which they happened.

A _____ I took a shower.

_____ I got out of bed.

_____ I got dressed.

B _____ She planted the seeds.

_____ Big pink flowers bloomed.

_____ Tiny green shoots came up.

C _____ He ate the sandwich.

_____ He spread some jelly on them.

_____ He got out two pieces of bread.

D _____ He slid down the slide.

_____ He climbed up the ladder.

_____ He landed on his feet.

E _____ Firefighters put out the fire.

_____ Lightning struck the barn.

_____ The barn caught on fire.

F _____ The pepper spilled out of the jar.

_____ I sneezed.

_____ My nose began to itch.

G _____ "My name is Emma."

_____ "Hi, what is your name?"

_____ "It's nice to meet you, Emma."

H _____ I said, "Okay, do a trick first."

_____ Rover whined for a treat.

_____ I gave him a dog biscuit.

_____ He danced on his hind legs.

I _____ She built a nest.

_____ Baby birds hatched from the eggs.

_____ I saw a robin gathering straw.

_____ She laid four blue eggs.

My Crazy Dream

I don't know why, but I went to school in my pajamas. Everyone was laughing!
I walked up and down the hall looking for my classroom, but I could never find it.
Then I went to the Lost and Found box and put on some clothes. I heard my principal say,
"Son, are you lost?" However, when I turned around, it was the president of the United
States talking to me. He asked me to fly on his jet with him. As we were flying, I looked out
the window and saw a pterodactyl flying next to us! How could that be? They are extinct!
It smiled and waved good-bye. Then all of a sudden, the airplane turned into a roller
coaster. It climbed upward a million miles, then down we went! For hours and hours, we
just kept going straight down! The roller coaster finally came to a stop, and I was on an
island made entirely of chocolate. I ate a whole tree made of fudge! Then a chef snuck up
and captured me. He put me in a pot of boiling water to make soup out of me. I got hotter
and hotter and hotter! Finally, I woke up and realized I had fallen asleep with my electric
blanket on high.

Number the pictures in the order that they happened in the dream.

Berry Colorful Ink

In early American schools, students used a quill pen and ink to practice writing letters and numerals. Since these schools did not have many supplies, the students often had to make their own ink at home. There were many different ways to make ink. One of the most common ways was to use berries such as blackberries, blueberries, cherries, elderberries, or strawberries. The type of berry used depended on the color of ink a student wanted. First, the type of berry to be used had to gathered. Then a strainer was filled with the berries and held over a bowl. Next, using the back of a wooden spoon, the berries were crushed. This caused the juice to strain into the bowl. After all the berry juice was strained into the bowl, salt and vinegar were added to the juice and then stirred. Finally, the juice was stored in a small jar with a tight-fitting lid. Not only did the students make colorful inks to use, they also made invisible and glow-in-the-dark inks.

> When sequencing a story, look for key words such as *first, then, next,* and *finally* to help you determine the correct sequence.

Number the phrases below in the order given in the story.

_____ The mixture was stirred.

_____ Using the back of a wooden spoon, the berries were crushed.

_____ The ink was stored in a small jar with a tight-fitting lid.

_____ Berries were gathered.

_____ All the berry juice was strained into the bowl.

_____ The strainer was held over a bowl.

_____ Salt and vinegar were added to the berry juice.

_____ A strainer was filled with berries.

 Look in a cookbook for a recipe you would like to try. Read all the steps. Have someone help you make the recipe. Be sure to follow each step in order.

Simon Says

When you play Simon Says, you only follow the directions that Simon says. You do not follow any other directions. Play the game following the directions below.

When **following directions**, it is important to read the directions carefully and to follow them in the order they are listed.

1 Simon says draw a hand in the box below.

2 Simon says draw fingernails on each finger.

3 Color each fingernail red.

4 Simon says write the names of five school days, one on each finger.

5 Write your teacher's name in the lower left-hand corner of the box.

6 Simon says write an addition problem on the hand, using the numbers 4, 5, and 9.

7 Simon says draw a watch on the wrist.

8 Simon says write your name in the top right-hand corner of the box.

Sneaky Snakes

Snakes are very good at **camouflage**. That means snakes use their colors and patterns to blend in with their surroundings. Camouflage helps them be **sneaky** when they are trying to capture food. For example, the emerald tree boa lives in the **rain forest**. Its green skin makes it nearly invisible among the leaves. **Rattlesnakes** live in rocky, dry places. Their black, tan, and brown patterns help them blend in with their environment. The horned viper lives in the desert. It has **sand**-colored skin. It is hard to see unless it is moving. Some harmless snakes look very similar to **venomous** snakes. The harmless milk snake is orange, with yellow and black stripes, much like the poisonous **coral snake**. Enemies of the milk snake mistake it for a coral snake because they look so much alike.

Find the answers in the story. Write them in the puzzle.

1 Write where emerald tree boas live.

2 Write the word that starts with a *v* and means "poisonous."

3 Write another word for "tricky."

4 Write what helps a snake blend in with its surroundings.

5 Write what snakes live in rocky places and have black, tan, and brown patterned skin.

6 Write what is the same color as the horned viper.

7 Write the name of the snake that looks like a milk snake.

Write the letter from the numbered squares in the puzzle above to fill in each box.

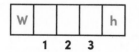   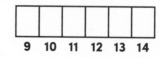 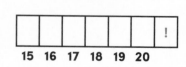

Fun With Words

Follow the directions to play each word game.

1 A palindrome is a word that is spelled the same forward or backward. Write each word backward. Circle each word that is a palindrome. Put an X on each word that is not.

wow _____

dad _____

mom _____

funny _____

noon _____

tall _____

deed _____

2 Homophones are words that sound alike when you say them but are spelled differently and have different meanings. For example, **see** and **sea** are homophones. Draw a line to match each pair of homophones.

knot   flew

right   soar

flu   not

sore   write

3 Some words imitate sounds. For example, the word "pop," sounds like a popping sound! That is called onomatopoeia. Unscramble each sound word. Write it correctly.

seechrc _____

owp _____

plurs _____

mobo _____

lckic _____

zzisel _____

chnucr _____

4 Add or subtract letters from each word to change it into another word. Write the new word.

peach – ch + r = _____

shirt – irt + oe = _____

love – ove + ike = _____

stove – st + n = _____

chicken – c – ick = _____

brother – bro + nei = _____

Where Is Holly?

One day, while Mom was washing dishes in the kitchen, she realized that she had not heard a peep out of three-year-old Holly in a long time. The last time she had seen her, she was playing in the living room with some building blocks. "She sure is being good," thought Mom.

Drawing conclusions means to make reasonable conclusions about events in a story using the information given.

Write an X next to the best answer.

1 Why did Mom think Holly was being good?

_____ **Holly was washing dishes for her.**

_____ **Holly was playing with dolls.**

_____ **Holly was being so quiet.**

After rinsing the last dish, Mom went to the living room to see what Holly had built. But Holly was not there. "Holly! Where are you?" Mom asked. Mom heard a faraway voice say, "Mommy!" So, Mom went outside to see if Holly was there.

2 Why did Mom go outside to look for Holly?

_____ **Holly's voice sounded so far away.**

_____ **The last time Mom saw Holly, she was riding her tricycle.**

_____ **Holly said, "I'm outside, Mommy."**

Mom looked down the street, up in the tree, and in the backyard, but Holly was not outside. She called her again but did not hear her voice. So, she went back inside. "Holly! Where are you? Come out right now."

3 Why did Mom say, "Come out right now"?

_____ She was mean.

_____ She heard Holly's voice coming from the closet.

_____ She thought Holly might be hiding.

Then, Mom heard "Help me!" She finally ran into Holly's room and saw her feet sticking out of the toy box. Mom lifted her out and asked, "Are you all right?" Holly replied, "I think so." Holly then told Mom that she had been looking for her toy piano because she wanted to play a song for her. "Do you want to hear it now?" Holly asked. "First, let's have a special snack. You can play the song for me later," Mom said.

4 Where was Holly's toy piano?

_____ The piano was under Holly's bed.

_____ The piano was at the bottom of the toy box.

_____ She was playing hide-and-seek with Mom.

Mom and Holly walked to the kitchen. Mom made Holly a bowl of ice cream with chocolate sauce and a cherry on top. Holly told Mom that she wanted to go to the park. Mom really liked that idea.

5 What will Mom and Holly do next?

_____ Mom and Holly will go shopping.

_____ Mom and Holly will go for a bike ride.

_____ Mom and Holly will go to the park.

Read a chapter from a book. Write a sentence telling what you think will happen next. Read the next chapter. Were you correct?

Potato Chips, Anyone?

Have you ever wondered who invented potato chips? Some people say George Crum was the first person to make them . . . by accident! In 1853, he was a chef at an elegant restaurant in Saratoga Springs, New York, called Moon's Lake House. A regular item on the menu was fried potatoes, which was an idea that had started in France. At that time, French fried potatoes were cut into thick slices. One day, a dinner guest at Moon's Lake House sent his fried potatoes back to the chef because he did not like them so thick. So, Mr. Crum cut the potatoes a little thinner and fried them. The guest did not like those either. That made Mr. Crum angry, so he thought he would just show that guy. He sliced the potatoes paper-thin and fried them, thinking that would hush the complaining diner. However, his plan backfired on him! The diner loved the crispy, thin potatoes! Other diners tried them and also liked them. So, Mr. Crum's potato chips were added to the menu. They were called Saratoga Chips. Eventually, Mr. Crum opened his own restaurant to sell his famous chips. Now potato chips are packaged and sold in grocery stores worldwide!

Draw a line to match each chip to a bag.

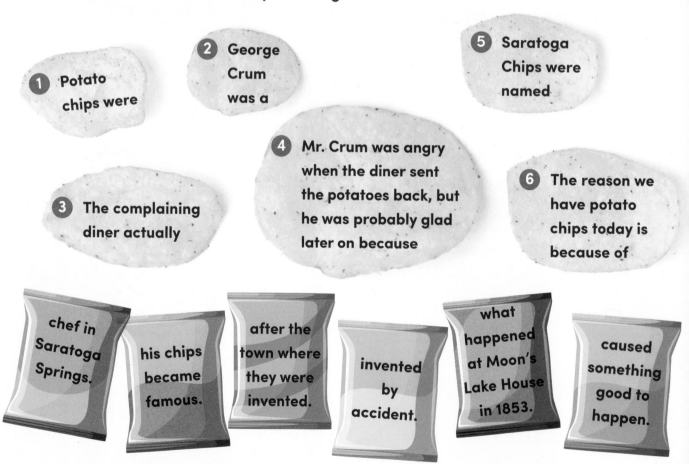

1. Potato chips were

2. George Crum was a

5. Saratoga Chips were named

4. Mr. Crum was angry when the diner sent the potatoes back, but he was probably glad later on because

3. The complaining diner actually

6. The reason we have potato chips today is because of

chef in Saratoga Springs.

his chips became famous.

after the town where they were invented.

invented by accident.

what happened at Moon's Lake House in 1853.

caused something good to happen.

Double It Up

Some words can share the same spelling but have completely different meanings. These words are called **homonyms**. To figure out the correct meaning of each word, use context clues. Using **context clues** means to look at the meaning of the whole sentence. One meaning for the word will make sense, and the other one will not. Read the following examples:

The bat flew out of the dark cave. (Would a baseball bat fly out of a cave? No. Then it must be the other kind of bat: a small flying animal.)

He swung the bat so hard that the ball went over the fence. (Would someone swing a small animal in order to hit a ball? Of course not!)

Picture each of the following sentences to help you decide which meaning is correct for each italicized word. Fill in the bubble next to the correct meaning.

1 I am sneezing because I have a *cold*.
○ opposite of hot
○ an illness

2 I rowed up to the *bank* and got out of the boat.
○ building where money is kept
○ shoreline of a river or creek

3 The garage is 15-*feet* wide.
○ a measurement
○ body parts used for walking

4 I like to put butter on my *roll*.
○ hot bread
○ to turn over and over

5 The *mouse* ran under the bushes.
○ a small, furry animal
○ hand control for a computer

6 Let's give the winner a big *hand*!
○ body part with fingers on it
○ applause

On another sheet of paper, write two sentences showing a different meaning for the word "star" in each.

A Family Camping Trip

Jemma and her family take an **annual** vacation. Every year, they go on a trip to a new and **distant** place. "Let's go to Forest Park and camp this year," said Jemma's father. "It's quiet and comfortable, and it's only a few hours from home.

Jemma likes Forest Park because of its **breathtaking** scenery. One amazing sight that excites her is the beautiful waterfall with its **perilous** drop of five hundred feet. Although Jemma delights in the beauty of the falls, she has to admit that the steepness of the drop also frightens her.

Jemma and her sisters love to hike in the **dense** forests where the pine trees are packed thickly together. When they reach a clearing, they watch the clouds sweep over their heads like waves on the ocean. At night, the stars shine brightly against the dark sky, like jewels laid out on a cloth of black velvet.

The campground is always **spotless**, too. People pick up their litter and carefully place it in trash cans. "This is a **wondrous** place," Jemma says. "It fills you with wonder about all of nature. The beauty of the place is so real and intense."

Often you can find the meaning of unfamiliar words by using **context clues**—the surrounding words and phrases. These clues help you determine what a new word means.

© Scholastic Inc.

Use context clues from the story to match each word with its definition.
Write the number of the word on the line.

1 breathtaking   _____ amazing; very beautiful

2 annual   _____ far away

3 dense   _____ clean

4 spotless   _____ dangerous

5 distant   _____ yearly

6 wondrous   _____ thick; crowded

7 perilous   _____ marvelous; full of wonder

Choose two words from above. Write the word and its definition.
Then, use each word in a sentence.

1 word _____ definition _____

sentence: _____

_____

2 word _____ definition _____

sentence: _____

_____

Read a chapter in a book. Use context clues in the story to determine the meaning of any unfamiliar words you come across.

Where Am I?

Read each riddle below. Look for clues to help you answer each question.

When you **make inferences** you use information in a story to make judgments about information not given in the story.

1 This thing keeps going faster and faster, up and down, and over and around. It tickles my tummy. The people behind me are screaming. I hope I don't go flying out of my seat! *Where am I?*

_____

2 Let's sit in the front row! Ha ha ha! That's funny . . . a cartoon about a drink cup that is singing to a candy bar. That makes me hungry. I think I'll go get some popcorn before it starts. *Where am I?*

_____

3 I can see rivers and highways that look like tiny ribbons. I am glad I got to sit by the window. Wow, we are in a cloud! "Yes, ma'am. I would like a drink. Thank you." *Where am I?*

_____

4 Doctor, can you help my dog? His name is Champ. He was bitten by a snake, and his leg is swollen. I hope he will be all right. *Where am I?*

_____

5 I am all dressed up, sitting here quietly with my parents. The flowers are pretty. The music is starting. Here she comes down the aisle. I wish they would hurry so I can have some cake! *Where am I?*

_____

6 This row has carrots growing, and this one has onions. The corn is getting tall. The soil feels dry. I better water the plants today. "Don't you think so, Mr. Scarecrow?" *Where am I?*

_____

 On another sheet of paper, write two "Where Am I?" riddles of your own. Read your riddles to someone else and have them guess where you are.

Moving In

The day we moved to our new house, there was a lot of work to do. Mom gave me the job of organizing the cabinets and closets. I unpacked each box and put things in their proper places. I filled up the medicine chest in the bathroom and the linen closet in the hall. I organized the silverware drawer in the kitchen, as well as the food in the pantry. I lined up Dad's stuff on the garage shelves. Last of all, I filled the bookshelf.

Write each word from the box in the correct category.

Medicine Chest	Linen Closet
_____	_____
_____	_____
_____	_____

Silverware Drawer	Pantry
_____	_____
_____	_____
_____	_____

Garage Shelves	Bookshelf
_____	_____
_____	_____
_____	_____

teaspoons
car wax
dictionary
cake mix
forks
atlas
aspirin
bandages
blankets
fishing tackle
crackers
novels
pillowcases
cereal
knives
sheets
toolbox
cough syrup

The Pyramid Game

Every morning before school, Mrs. Cavazos writes four words inside a pyramid on the chalkboard. When class begins, her students are to think of a title for the group of words. The title is to tell how the words are alike.

Write a title for each pyramid of words.

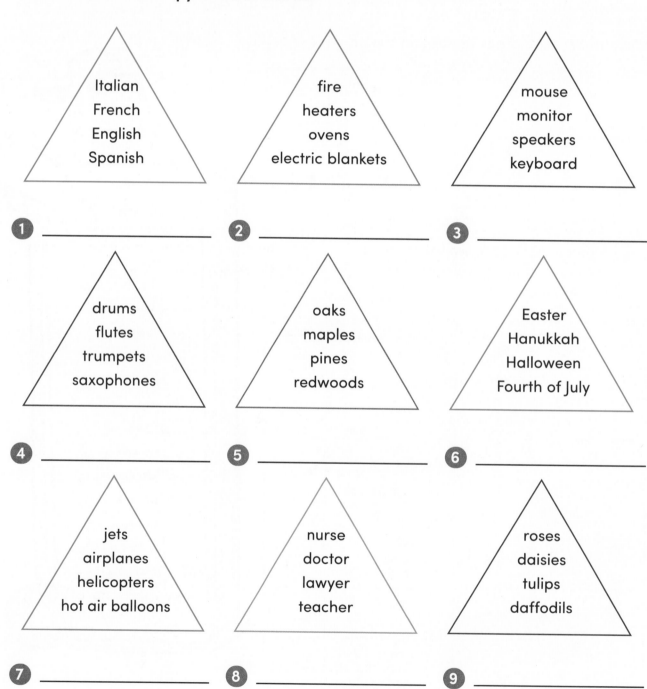

Italian
French
English
Spanish

1 _____

fire
heaters
ovens
electric blankets

2 _____

mouse
monitor
speakers
keyboard

3 _____

drums
flutes
trumpets
saxophones

4 _____

oaks
maples
pines
redwoods

5 _____

Easter
Hanukkah
Halloween
Fourth of July

6 _____

jets
airplanes
helicopters
hot air balloons

7 _____

nurse
doctor
lawyer
teacher

8 _____

roses
daisies
tulips
daffodils

9 _____

News or Views?

When people talk about things, they often mix news with opinions. Read each cartoon. Write *News* in the box if it is a fact. Write *Views* in the box if it is a person's own personal opinion.

Facts are true statements and can be proven. **Opinions** are a person's own personal views or beliefs.

1 Punky Starr is the best rock singer that ever lived!

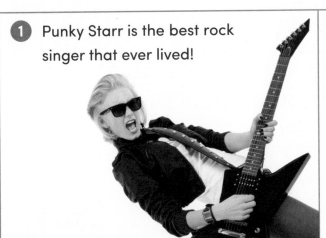

2 Oranges were 3 for $1.00 at the Farmer's Market today.

3 When it gets dark, we will be able to see the Big Dipper and the North Star!

4 The city council will meet on Monday to vote on the new highway.

5 Ha ha ha ha! This show is funny!

6 The math homework for today is on page 34.

TV Commercials

When you watch TV, you see a lot of commercials advertising different products. The people making the commercial want you to buy their product, so they make it sound as good as possible. Some of the things they say are facts, which can be proven. Other things are just the advertiser's opinion about how good the product is or how it will make you feel.

Read each advertisement below. Write an _F_ in the box beside each fact and an _O_ in the box beside each opinion. The first one is done for you.

Drive an XJ-80 Sports Car today.

[O] You'll never want to drive your old car again.

[F] available in black, red, and silver

Get a Pair of Extreme In-Line Skates!

[ ] You'll be the coolest kid on your block.

[ ] on sale for $79.99

Sky-Diving Adventure Video Game

[ ] joystick sold separately

[ ] You'll have hours and hours of fun!

Elastic Man, the Movie

[ ] full of heart-stopping action and mind-blowing special effects

[ ] "this year's best motion picture"

[ ] starring Academy Award-winning actor Stretch Hamstring

[ ] now showing at the new Movie Town Theater

[ ] rated PG

Small-Town Tornado

Read the following details about a tornado that touched down in a small town in Oklahoma. If the sentence is a fact that can be proven, underline it in red. If the sentence is someone's opinion, highlight it in yellow.

1. At 10:35 A.M. today, a tornado touched down briefly in the small town of Parksville, Oklahoma.

2. The roofs of several buildings were torn off by the strong winds.

3. Many large trees were uprooted.

4. There were no injuries.

5. "It was so loud, I thought a freight train was coming right through my living room!" Mrs. Cox exclaimed.

6. The National Weather Service issued a warning ten minutes before the tornado hit.

7. "I was afraid my house was going to blow away!" Mr. Carey reported.

8. Officer Reeves commented, "This may have been the worst day in the history of Parksville."

9. Power was out for over two hours.

10. The large scoreboard at the football field was blown down.

 On another sheet of paper, write a news report about a topic of your choice. Include three facts and three opinions.

Homer's Big Adventure

Brian was in such a hurry to get to the school bus on time that he forgot to close the door on Homer's cage after he fed him. Homer T. Hamster knew this was his big chance. He crawled out of his cage and ran downstairs, careful to sneak past Brian's mother without being seen. He ducked through a hole in the screen door and stepped out into the great backyard.

"Yippeeee!" cried Homer, throwing his little arms into the air. "I'm free at last!" He zipped through the gate and down the alley. The first thing Homer saw was a huge, snarling German shepherd who thought it was fun to chase anything that could run. "R-r-ruff! R-r-ruff!"

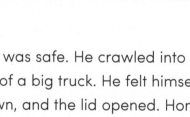

Homer scurried here and there, only inches ahead of the dog. He barely escaped by hiding under a flowerpot. "Whew, that was close!" he thought. He waited there awhile, shaking like a leaf.

Then he crept out into the alley again. He looked this way and that. The coast was clear, so he skipped happily along. He looked up just in time to see the big black tires of a pickup truck that was backing out of a driveway. He almost got squooshed! So, he darted quickly into someone's backyard where a boy was mowing the lawn. R-r-r-r-r-r! Homer had to jump out of the way again.

Back in the alley, he decided to rest somewhere that was safe. He crawled into a garbage dumpster and fell asleep. Later, he heard the sound of a big truck. He felt himself going high up into the air. The dumpster turned upside down, and the lid opened. Homer was falling. "Yikes!" screamed Homer. He had to think fast. He reached out and grabbed the side of the truck, holding on for dear life.

The truck rolled down the alley and into the street. As it turned the corner, Homer was flung off the truck and onto the hood of a school bus. He grabbed onto the windshield wipers as the bus drove to the corner and stopped.

The bus driver exclaimed, "Look, kids! There is a hamster riding on our bus!" All the kids rushed forward to see the funny sight. Homer looked through the windshield at all the surprised faces. All of a sudden, Homer saw Brian! Brian ran out of the bus and carefully picked up Homer. "Hey, buddy, how did you get out here? Are you okay?" Brian asked as he petted Homer's fur.

1 What do you think happened next? Color the picture that seems to be the most likely ending to the story.

2 Underline the sentence that tells the main idea of the story.
- Homer hid under a flowerpot to escape from a German shepherd.
- Homer had many exciting adventures after crawling out of his cage.
- Brian was surprised to see Homer riding the school bus.

3 Do you think Homer will leave his cage again? Write a sentence to tell why or why not.

_____

_____

Mary's Mystery

Monday afternoon, Mom called my sister, Mary, to the door. The florist had just delivered flowers to her. "For me?" asked Mary. "Who would be sending me flowers?" Mom told her to read the card. It said, "You are the best! Thanks for your help." Mary looked puzzled. She could not think of anyone that she had helped recently.

On the following Wednesday, a delivery person brought a package to the door. He said, "This is for Mary." It was a box of chocolates. Mary liked chocolate very much, but she could not figure out who was sending her gifts, or why. The box also came with a note. It said, "You did it again. You're truly amazing!"

On Friday, another delivery person came to the door. He asked, "Are you Mary?" She nodded her head and said, "Yes." Then, the man handed her an envelope. Inside were two tickets for a concert that night.

That evening, a young woman came to the door. Mary opened the door. When the woman saw Mary, she looked surprised. She said, "Oh, I'm sorry. I was looking for Mary's apartment." Mary said, "Well, I am Mary." The woman stood there frowning for a moment. Then she started to laugh.

"No wonder my friend has not mentioned the gifts I sent. I bet they have all been coming here." Then she told Mary to step outside and look at the metal numbers over her apartment door. Mary's apartment was #620, but the 6 had come loose and had turned upside down. That made it look like #920. The woman said, "I am sorry about the mix-up. My friend, Mary, just moved into apartment #920. I think all the delivery people saw your #920 and stopped here, just like I did. I guess when they found out your name was Mary, they thought they had the right place." Mary laughed. "Now I understand," she said. "I already ate the chocolates, but here are the tickets. I hope you and your friend enjoy the concert." The woman replied, "That's okay." Then as she turned to walk away she added, "You can also keep the flowers."

1 Underline two sentences below that tell what might happen next. Mark an X on the sentence that tells about something that probably will not happen.

The woman found the other Mary, her friend, and told her what had happened.

The woman sent Mary a bill because she ate the chocolates.

Mary's mom turned the 9 over to make a 6 again and nailed it tight so their apartment number would be correct.

2 What did the florist deliver to Mary? _____

3 Which gift do you think Mary liked the best? Why?_____

_____

4 On what day did Mary receive the concert tickets? _____

5 Where is the setting of this story? _____

On another sheet of paper, write a paragraph telling what you think the two friends will do that evening.

Special Charts

To **compare** and **contrast** means to show the similarities and differences of things. A Venn diagram is a chart made of overlapping circles that can be used to organize the similarities and differences. The overlapping parts of the circles show how things are similar. The other part of the circles show how things are different.

Joe, Kim, and Rob each got a lunch tray, went through the lunch line, and sat together to eat. These students all had the same lunch menu, but each one only ate what he or she liked. Joe ate chicken nuggets, green beans, applesauce, and carrots. Rob ate chicken nuggets, green beans, a roll, and corn. Kim ate chicken nuggets, a roll, applesauce, and salad.

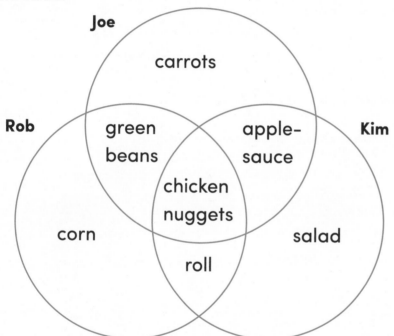

1. What did all three students eat? _____

2. What did Joe and Rob eat that Kim did not? _____

3. What did Kim and Rob eat that Joe did not? _____

4. What did Joe eat that no one else ate? _____

5. What did Kim eat that no one else ate? _____

Sports Chart

There are three brothers who love to play sports. Each one is good at several different sports. Jeff plays hockey, football, soccer, and baseball. Allen plays hockey, football, tennis, and golf. Seth plays hockey, tennis, soccer, and basketball.

Complete the Venn diagram showing which sports each brother plays. Start with the sport all three brothers have in common. Write it in the shared space of all three circles.

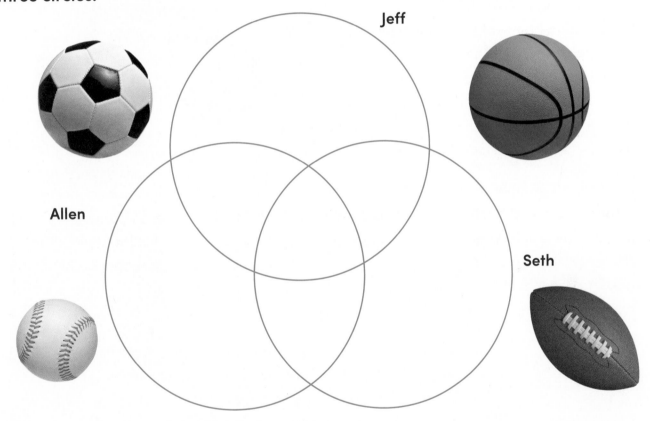

1 What sport do all three boys like to play? _____

2 What sport do Jeff and Allen like to play that Seth does not? _____

3 What sport do Allen and Seth like to play that Jeff does not? _____

4 What sport does Jeff like to play that no one else does? _____

5 What sport does Allen like to play that no one else does? _____

Sharks

There are over 400 different kinds of sharks. The whale shark is the largest. It is as big as a whale. The dwarf lantern is the smallest. It is less than seven inches long.

All sharks live in the ocean, which is salt water, but a few kinds can swim from salt water to fresh water. Bull sharks have been found in the Mississippi River!

Sharks do not have bones. They have skeletons made of cartilage, which is the same thing your ears and nose are made of. A shark's skin is made of spiky, hard scales. The jaws of a shark are very powerful. When a great white shark bites, it clamps down on its prey and thrashes its head from side to side. It is the deadliest shark.

Sharks eat fish, dolphins, and seals. The tiger shark will eat just about anything. Some fishermen have discovered unopened cans of food, clocks, boat cushions, and even a keg of nails inside tiger sharks. Sometimes sharks even eat other sharks. For example, a tiger shark might eat a bull shark. The bull shark might have eaten a blacktip shark. The blacktip shark might have eaten a dogfish shark. So a tiger shark could be found with three sharks in its stomach!

Some sharks look very unusual. The hammerhead shark has a head shaped somewhat like a hammer, with eyes set very far apart. A cookie cutter shark has a circular set of teeth. When it bites a dolphin or whale, it leaves a perfectly round hole in its victim. The sawshark has a snout with sharp teeth on the outside, which makes it look like a saw. The goblin shark has a sharp-pointed spear coming out of its head, and its ragged teeth make it look scary!

The mako shark is the fastest swimmer. Sometimes mako sharks have been known to leap out of the water, right into a boat! These are just a few of the many kinds of fascinating sharks.

Complete the chart with the name of the
correct shark. If the statement is about all
sharks, write *all*.

	whale shark
1 the largest shark	
2 the smallest shark	
3 the deadliest shark	
4 the fastest swimmer	
5 live in the ocean	
6 have skeletons of cartilage	
7 has a sharp-pointed spear coming out of its head	
8 has a head shaped like a hammer	
9 skin of spiky, hard scales	
10 leaves a round bite mark	
11 looks like a saw	
12 has eaten unopened cans, clocks, and boat cushions	

Read more about two different kinds of sharks. On another sheet of
paper, list two similarities and two differences.

Earthquake!

Earthquakes are one of the most powerful events on Earth.
When large sections of underground rock break and move
suddenly, an earthquake occurs. This causes the
ground to shake back and forth. Small earthquakes
do not cause much damage, but large ones do. Some
earthquakes have caused buildings and bridges to
fall. Others have caused rivers to change their paths.
Earthquakes near mountains and cliffs can cause
landslides that cover up the houses and roads below.
If a large earthquake occurs under the ocean, it can
cause giant waves which flood the seashore. When
large earthquakes occur in a city, there is danger of
fire from broken gas lines and electric lines. Damaged
roads make it difficult for rescue workers to get to
people who need help. Scientists are trying to find ways to
predict when an earthquake will happen so that people can be warned ahead of time.

> The **cause** in a
> story is what made
> something happen.
> The **effect** is what
> happened.

Draw a shaky line under each correct effect.

Earthquakes can cause . . .

1. landslides
2. tornadoes
3. fire from broken gas and electric lines
4. huge waves that flood the seashore
5. swarms of flies

6. buildings and bridges to fall
7. sunburns
8. rivers to change their paths
9. damaged roads
10. lightning

 Read about tornadoes. On another sheet of paper, make a list of eight
things a tornado might cause.

Good News for Bears?

Thousands of grizzly bears once roamed the western U.S. But in the 1800s, settlers began building homes and farms on the land where the bears lived. Grizzlies had less room to roam. Out of fear, settlers also hunted the bears.

Yellowstone National Park is in Wyoming and parts of Montana and Idaho. It became one of the few places in the U.S. with a grizzly bear population. By 1975, only 136 grizzlies were left there.

That's when the U.S. government added the bears to its list of protected animals. Being on the list meant that people could no longer hunt them or harm their habitat. Now, about 700 grizzlies live in and around Yellowstone.

Then, in 2017, the government decided to take Yellowstone's grizzlies off the list of protected animals. Not everyone was happy. Some wildlife groups, like the Sierra Club, took the government to court. They wanted the government to change its decision.

It could take years for the courts to decide whether the grizzlies should be back on the list. Until then, Bonnie Rice of the Sierra Club hopes that the government keeps a close eye on the bears.

Use the chart below to find the cause-and-effect relationships in the article.

Cause (why something happens)		Effect (what happens as a result)
Grizzly bears weren't on the list of endangered species.	→	_____
_____	→	*The number of grizzly bears in and around Yellowstone National Park has grown.*

Nonfiction: A Biography

Steve Irwin

Steve Irwin was a famous TV personality and **reptile** specialist from **Australia**. People knew him as the **Crocodile Hunter**.

Steve's parents, Bob and Lyn Irwin, owned a reptile park. Steve grew up learning about and handling reptiles, as well as many other kinds of **animals**. When Steve was six years old, his father gave him a snake called a scrub **python**. Steve named it **Fred**. Steve's dad taught him all about the **wildlife** of Australia and took him on field trips to study about it. Steve often begged to go on these field trips rather than go to school. He caught his first crocodile when he was only nine years old.

Steve ran the Australia **Zoo**. He was a **herpetologist**. That means he was a reptile **expert**. His mission in life was to educate people about animals, teaching them to treat even dangerous animals with **respect**. Steve never hurt animals. In fact, he rescued many animals that were in **danger**, especially crocodiles. Steve was an expert snake handler. He held them by the tail and let them go safely. He always warned others, though, that picking up a **snake** is very dangerous.

Steve married an American named **Terri**. She helped Steve handle the animals. They had a daughter named **Bindi** and a son named Robert. Steve Irwin died in 2006 while filming a TV show about dangerous animals.

A **biography** is the story of a person's life. You have probably read biographies of presidents or famous people in history. The biography on this page is about one of the most popular zookeepers of our time.

Look at the bolded words in the story. Find each word in the puzzle and circle it. The words may go up, down, forward, backward, or diagonally.

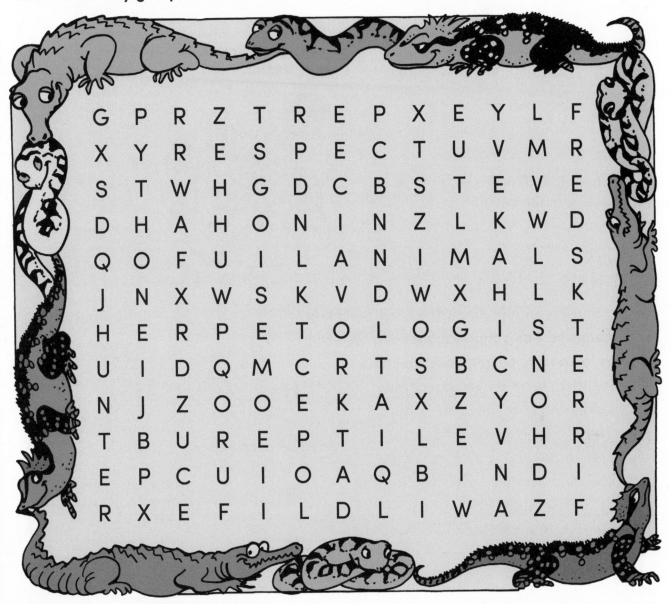

```
G P R Z T R E P X E Y L F
X Y R E S P E C T U V M R
S T W H G D C B S T E V E
D H A H O N I N Z L K W D
Q O F U I L A N I M A L S
J N X W S K V D W X H L K
H E R P E T O L O G I S T
U I D Q M C R T S B C N E
N J Z O O E K A X Z Y O R
T B U R E P T I L E V H R
E P C U I O A Q B I N D I
R X E F I L D L I W A Z F
```

List two facts about Steve Irwin.

1 _____

2 _____

 Find the biography section in the library. Check out a biography about someone who had a career that interests you.

Acrostic Poems

Acrostic poetry is fun. An **acrostic poem** starts with a word that is the subject of the whole poem. The word is written vertically. Then, words or phrases about that subject are written using each letter. Look at the example below.

Sleeping late

Under the ceiling fan

May we go to the pool?

My, it's hot!

Eating watermelon

Relaxing on vacation

Now it is your turn! Finish each acrostic poem below by writing something about the word that is written vertically, using each letter of the word.

T_____

E lementary school

A_____

C_____

H elps me learn

E_____

R_____

H_____

O ats for dinner

R_____

S_____

E_____

S addle them up!

 On another sheet of paper, make an acrostic poem about yourself. Start by writing your name vertically

ANSWER KEY

Page 6
1. Alexander Graham Bell
2. "Mr. Watson, come here! I want to see you!"
3. Mr. Bell's assistant
4. Bell showed his invention to many people.

Page 7
Main Idea: The Milky Way is our galaxy.
Details: A galaxy is a grouping of **stars**.
There are many other galaxies in **outer** space.
It is a **spiral**-shaped galaxy.
The Milky Way looks like a milky **white** stripe in the sky.
One of the stars in the Milky Way is the **sun**.
Some scientists believe there are hundreds of **billions** of stars in the Milky Way.

Page 8
Life on a wagon train was hard and dangerous.
1. gathering
2. cooking
3. waiting
4. watching
5. crossing
6. getting

Page 9
Main Idea: Elephants have very useful noses.
Sentence that does not belong: Giraffes are the tallest animals in the world. (The rest of the sentences are details.)

Page 10
1. Mr. Jefferson, Riley, Rhonda
2. in Mr. Jefferson's classroom
3. Class was almost over, and the contest was still tied.
4. Riley

Page 11
Check drawings.

Page 13
1. B   2. E, A, D
3. G   4. C
5. F

Page 14
1. land by the sea
2. weather
3. happens regularly
4. outer covering of trees
5. illness
6. wood cut into boards
7. no longer existing

Page 15

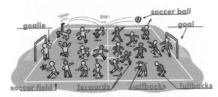

Page 16
A. 2, 1, 3   B. 1, 3, 2
C. 3, 2, 1   D. 2, 1, 3
E. 3, 1, 2   F. 1, 3, 2
G. 2, 1, 3   H. 2, 1, 4, 3
I. 2, 4, 1, 3

Page 17
4, 6, 1, 3, 5, 2

Page 18
7, 4, 8, 1, 5, 3, 6, 2

Page 19
Check pages.

Page 20
1. rain forest
2. venomous
3. sneaky
4. camouflage
5. rattlesnakes
6. sand
7. coral snake
Watch out for sneaky snakes!

Page 21
1. The palindromes are wow, dad, mom, noon, deed. (The other words are not.)
2. knot–not, flu–flew, sore–soar, right–write
3. screech, pow, slurp, boom, click, sizzle, crunch
4. pear, shoe, like, oven, hen, neither

Pages 22–23
1. Holly was being so quiet.
2. Holly's voice sounded so far away.
3. She thought Holly might be hiding.
4. The piano was at the bottom of the toy box.
5. Mom and Holly will go to the park.

Page 24
1. Potato chips were invented by accident.
2. George Crum was a chef in Saratoga Springs.
3. The complaining diner actually caused something good to happen.
4. Mr. Crum was angry when the diner sent the potatoes back, but he was probably glad later on because his chips became famous.
5. Saratoga Chips were named after the town where they were invented.
6. The reason we have potato chips today is because of what happened at Moon's Lake House in 1853.

Page 25
1. an illness
2. shoreline of a river or creek
3. a measurement
4. hot bread
5. a small, furry animal
6. applause

Page 27
1. amazing; very beautiful
2. yearly
3. thick; crowded
4. clean
5. far away
6. marvelous; full of wonder
7. dangerous
Answers will vary.

Page 28
1. on a roller coaster
2. at a movie
3. on an airplane
4. at the vet
5. at a wedding
6. in a garden

Page 29
Medicine Chest: aspirin, cough syrup, bandages
Linen Closet: blankets, sheets, pillowcases
Silverware Drawer: forks, knives, teaspoons
Pantry: cereal, crackers, cake mix
Garage Shelves: toolbox, fishing tackle, car wax
Bookshelf: dictionary, novels, atlas

Page 30
Wording of answers may vary:
1. Kinds of Languages
2. Things That Are Hot
3. Computer Equipment
4. Musical Instruments
5. Kinds of Trees
6. Holidays
7. Air Transportation
8. Careers (or Occupations)
9. Kinds of Flowers

Page 31
1. views 2. news 3. news
4. news 5. views 6. news

Page 32
In-line Skates: O, F
Video Game: F, O
Movie: O, O, F, F, F

Page 33
Facts: 1, 2, 3, 4, 6, 9, 10
Opinions: 5, 7, 8

Page 35
1. The picture of Homer in his cage should be colored.
2. Homer had many exciting adventures after crawling out of his cage.
3. Answers will vary.

Page 37
1. **Underline:** The woman found the other Mary, her friend, and told her what had happened. Mary's mom turned the 9 over to make a 6 again and nailed it tight so their apartment number would be correct.
Mark an X on: The woman sent Mary a bill because she ate the chocolates.
2. flowers
3. Answers will vary.
4. Friday
5. Mary's apartment

Page 38
1. chicken nuggets
2. green beans
3. roll
4. carrots
5. salad

Page 39

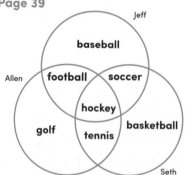

Jeff
baseball
Allen
football   soccer
hockey
golf   tennis   basketball
Seth

1. hockey 2. football 3. tennis
4. baseball 5. golf

Page 41
1. whale shark
2. dwarf lantern shark
3. great white shark
4. mako shark
5. all
6. all
7. goblin shark
8. hammerhead shark
9. all
10. cookie cutter shark
11. sawshark
12. tiger shark

Page 42
1, 3, 4, 6, 8, 9

Page 43
Effect: The grizzly bear population shrank.
Cause: The government decided to add Yellowstone's grizzlies to the list of protected animals.

Page 45

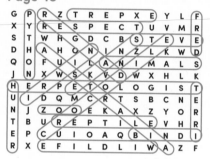

Facts will vary.

Page 46
Answers will vary.